LEAD WITH YOUR LIFE

LEAD WITH YOUR LIFE

7 PRINCIPLES OF LEADERS

BY

ALMON W. GUNTER, JR.

A BOOK IN THE SUPER FREAK
WAY SERIES

Lead with Your Life: 7 Principles of Leadership
Copyright © 2019 Almon Gunter Motivates, Inc.
All rights reserved. No portion of this book may be reproduced, stored in a retrieval system, or transmitted in any form or by any means—electronic, mechanical, photocopying, recording, or by any information storage or retrieval system—except for brief quotations in printed reviews without prior permission from Almon Gunter Motivates, Inc.
Book design by Creative Services, Inc., Sewanee, Tennessee 37375
Cover design by Greg Dorsey
ISBN: 978-0-9993266-2-6

Printed in the United States of America and other locations.

For information or to request authorization to make copies of any part of this work contact
Almon Gunter Motivates, Inc.
Post Office Box 194
Jacksonville, Florida 32234
Phone 904.803.1917
Web Address: www.almongunterexperience.com
Email: almon@almonguntermotivates.com
Twitter: @almongunter
Facebook: Almon Gunter
Istagram: almongunter
LinkedIn: Almon W Gunter Jr

Dedication

This book is dedicated to my mother Eunice M. Gunter, my father Almon W. Gunter Sr., my stepfather Fredrick Shellman, my aunt Edna R. Brown, my uncle Lawrence G. Gunter, my paternal grandparents Wilson and Louisa Gunter, and my maternal grandparents Levi and Ronita Shannon. I am so blessed to have had excellent leadership modeled for me each and every day of my life.

CONTENTS

DEDICATION

FOREWORD   1

INTRODUCTION   3

CHAPTER 1
PEOPLE OF CHARACTER   11

CHAPTER 2
VISIONARIES   22

CHAPTER 3
COMMUNICATING THE VISION   31

CHAPTER 4
COMPETENCIES   41

CHAPTER 5
PEOPLE SKILLS   50

CHAPTER 6
BOLD BEHAVIORS   58

CHAPTER 7
SERVANT LEADERS   66

SUMMARY   75

ABOUT THE AUTHOR   79

ACKNOWLEDGMENTS   80

Foreword

Many people and their accomplishments come to mind when we consider the word "leadership." Names like Lincoln, M.L. King, Jr., Gandhi, Churchill, Winfrey, Gates, and Bezos echo in the halls of great leadership. Perhaps thoughts of herculean efforts yielding monumental outcomes like Mount Rushmore, the Great Wall, the splitting of an atom, or the birth of a new nation conceived in liberty most effectively manifest the results of great leadership.

Efforts to learn about the tenets of leadership will likely lead to such historical luminaries and their endeavors. These individuals' lives exemplify the truth that no great result has ever been achieved without great leadership.

But what about the leadership needed every day in business, sports, faith, family, and the classroom? Can the same principles that guided great historical leaders be applied to a small team on the field or in the workplace? Fortunately, the answer is, Yes!

As a veteran of adult education, business management, and leadership, I have had the opportunity to collaborate with incredible leaders of business and industry and to lead some amazing teams to achieve incredible results. None of these could have been achieved without practicing the leadership principles so clearly and eloquently presented by Almon Gunter in this book.

Almon's *The Super Freak Way* book series is a must-read collection for all who seek to improve their own leadership abilities regardless of their areas of endeavor. *Lead with Your Life* is yet another awesome collection of truths, principles, analogies, and examples that when applied will greatly improve your understanding of true leadership and how it should be practiced.

More than writing a manual of what to "do," Almon provides great insights into and practical examples of how leaders should "be." By living, modeling, and demonstrating the 7 critical principles discussed in this book, you can become a great leader. I encourage you to read this book with an open mind and a willingness to challenge your own previous perceptions of what great leadership is. Whether you are a veteran of management and leadership or just beginning your journey, this book will serve as a great first step or your best next step to becoming a great leader.

—John-Michael Castillo
Educator, Speaker, Author

Introduction

"To every man there comes in his lifetime a special moment when he is figuratively tapped on the shoulder and offered a chance to do a very special thing, unique to him and fitted to his talents. What a tragedy if that moment finds him unprepared or unqualified for that which would become his finest hour."

—*Winston Churchill, prime minister of the United Kingdom from 1940 to 1945 and from 1951 to 1955, led Britain to victory in the Second World War.*

If you haven't read my previous books, you're probably wondering what I mean by "The Super Freak Way" on this book's title page. Super Freaks study and learn from the best leaders. While they steadily pursue their own dreams, Super Freaks help those they lead to maximize their potential. Because Super Freaks dedicate themselves to helping others, they are called "servant leaders." Super Freaks are result driven, and the results are always positive. The Super Freak Way is the way we choose to live our lives.

Leadership is defined as the position or function of a leader, a person who guides or directs a group. Leadership is first and foremost a set of actions and not a position. A leader has the ability to turn people on, inspire them beyond any reasonable doubt, and get 100-percent effort out of the relationship while pursuing a common objective. Leaders serve their people by helping them remove obstacles that may hinder their progress personally and professionally. Leaders provide all of the necessary tools individuals need to be successful regardless of their field of endeavor. Successful leaders are always available, accessible, and willing to hear the voices of the people they serve and then take the right actions for the best possible solutions. Great leaders' open-door policy is obvious to the people they lead, because these leaders remove the doors to their offices figuratively and literally.

Great leaders promote healthy competition and accept clashes of ideas to move individuals, the family, school, team, organization, or business forward. A leader understands that ideas are the heart and soul of every group, and ideas can build an organization or destroy it. Successful leaders continually look for great ideas no matter who has the ideas. Great leaders surround themselves with people who are energetic, bright, and capable of being in charge at a moment's notice. Outstanding leaders know how to pick the right people and develop them to reach 100 percent of their potential. After all, the best people will have the best ideas and finish what they start. Therefore, strong leaders surround themselves with innovative people who can walk the talk.

Outstanding leaders listen, simplify, and pay close attention to the details of their people and their organization. They have one true pipeline of communication: They define their expectations clearly and expect everyone to comply. Outstanding leaders execute and master all of the details necessary for hitting the mark. Successful leaders create an environment that operates with a common language and a message of one vision, one mission, and one goal. They strive every day to make sure that everyone on the team is on the same page, reading, understanding, speaking, listening, and executing the same information at the same time.

When you, as a leader, *Lead with Your Life*, you embody seven principles that will inspire and motivate those you lead. These principles allow the leader to walk his or her talk daily and to lead with his or her life. The following principles help shape, define, and account for leaders' overall success: People of Character, Visionaries, Communicating the

Vision, Competencies, People Skills, Bold Behaviors, and Servant Leaders. When these seven principles are consistently part of an individual leader's actions, the end result will always be outstanding leadership that individuals will gladly follow.

Super Freaks' Outline of the 7 Principles of Leadership

1. People of Character: Outstanding leaders are people of character. Individuals who are compelled to do what they say they will do are people with high moral values. It is important as a leader to model the attitudes, behaviors, and actions you want to see in others. People of character adopt the perspective that there is enough for everyone if we each just do our part. Leadership isn't a popularity contest. Successful leaders are ultimately the people who inspire others to maximize their potential. Leaders encourage others, become constant resources, and serve each team member every step of the way. Great leaders get great results from the people they lead. They inspire not by words alone but by their actions. Great leaders model the way and always lead with their lives.

> "People of character do the right thing even if no one else does, not because they think it will change the world but because they refuse to be changed by the world."
>
> —*Michael Josephson, founder of the Josephson Institute of Ethics.*

2. Visionaries: Outstanding leaders are visionaries. They have a sense of mission and purpose or, as I like to say, they know what they are playing for daily. Great leaders can visualize future results, yet they stay in the moment and do the little things. Leaders who have vision work with incredible imaginations and thoughtful insights. They build bridges for others to cross and know how to develop winning teams. They present a challenge that calls forth the best in people and brings them together around a shared sense of purpose and understanding. They work with the power of intentionality and are driven to fulfill a higher purpose. Visionary leaders' eyes are always on the horizon, as well as what is near at hand. They have the ability to see further than their eyes can look. Outstanding leaders are innovators and agents for change for all. They see the big picture and think strategically.

> "Don't underestimate the power of your vision to change the world. Whether that world is your office, your community, an industry or a global movement, you need to have a core belief that what you contribute can fundamentally change the paradigm or way of thinking about problems."
>
> —Leroy Hood, biologist who invented instruments related to DNA.

3. Communicating the Vision: Outstanding leaders communicate their vision with optimism and hope to every member of the team. Great leaders are salespersons of the art of possibilities. Outstanding leaders know the right words to speak to their teams not only at the right time but every time. More importantly, exceptional leaders let their actions inspire the masses by walking the talk. Their actions and words constantly paint a picture that all members of an organization can see and embrace as their own. Great leaders model the way for others to follow each day.

> "People need to see a vision to connect with it, which is why the great communicators harness imagery to amplify the power of their message. Storytelling gets much more mileage than fact-spewing. However, the best representation of a vision occurs when a leader embodies it. People sooner follow what they see than what they hear. When a leader is ablaze with passion, people invariably are attracted to the flame."
>
> —John C. Maxwell, author, speaker, pastor, and coach, was called America's No. 1 leadership authority and was identified by Inc. magazine, in 2014, as the most popular leadership expert in the world.

4. Competencies: Outstanding leaders are competent in their abilities to lead their teams to success. Being competent is knowing the job and knowing what it takes to maximize the potential of everyone on the team. Competent leaders don't claim to have all of the answers; however, they utilize every resource that is available to them to make sure that all members of the team have what they need to be successful. They do what they say they will do, which creates trust and respect between leadership and the frontline workers. Competent leaders aren't afraid to make mistakes. They hold themselves in the same high regard as they hold each team member. Outstanding leaders, through consistency, communication, and follow-up, create an environment of trust and respect throughout the organization, family, school, business, or team. Competent leaders know how to find, create, and utilize all of their own and their team's resources.

"Excellence is not a singular act; it's a habit. You are what you repeatedly do."

—*Aristotle (384–322 BC), a great philosopher and the first person to identify several scientific fields.*

5. People Skills: Outstanding leaders have incredible people skills. They encourage each member on the team to tap into his or her purpose and dare to be great. The simplest definition of the word "empower" is to enable or to permit. In other words, when we empower others we simply let go. We allow others to do what they say they can do. Letting go is much easier said than done for many of us as we pursue our goals. As a teammate, leader, parent, student, or teacher, permitting or allowing others to pursue their dreams can be challenging and difficult because it requires us to let go and to trust those we lead to make decisions. After all, who really wants to put his or her hopes and dreams in the hands of someone else?

Great leaders and great teams have the ability to let go and let all members execute their roles for the good of the team. Outstanding leaders possess the faith needed to give their all for the possibility that those they lead will become champions.

> "Skill at helping people grow mentally, physically, spiritually, economically, socially, etcetera, like skill at playing chess, depends on understanding and valuing differences."
>
> —*John Ortberg, senior pastor at Menlo Presbyterian Church, psychologist, and author.*

6. Bold Behaviors: Outstanding leaders are bold in all that they do. Being bold means being able to be decisive. It means having the ability to make a decision and stick with it. Great leaders decide it, say it, and then do it. They don't second-guess or beat themselves up over the decisions they have made. Outstanding leaders are comfortable standing in the fire. They understand the truism: "The hottest fire produces the strongest steel." They are extremely confident in their ability to produce their desired results. Many times confidence in one's own ability may be mistaken for arrogance; however, as my college track coach Larry Monts would say, "It ain't bragging if you can do it." People who achieve major successes do so because of their assertiveness and passion for what they believe in. Simply stated, they just do the work required to reach their goal day in and day out. Outstanding leaders don't take plays off. They don't lack effort in any way. Successful leaders want what they want, and they are not only willing to pay the price to get it, they gladly pay the price every day.

> "It is better by noble boldness to run the risk of being subject to half the evils we anticipate than to remain in cowardly listlessness for fear of what might happen."
>
> —*Herodotus (circa 484–425 BC), Greek historian who wrote* The Histories, *a study of the causes of of the Greco-Persian Wars*

7. Servant Leaders: Outstanding leaders are servants. Great leaders understand that the most valuable asset of any family, organization, team, business, or school is the people. Without people who are inspired and motivated, at the end of the day, you have a great product or service that no one knows about. Outstanding leaders serve their people daily. They supply the resources needed for each individual to reach his or her maximum potential. Outstanding leaders also listen to their people and actually hear what they are saying. They get results by planning properly and then executing the plan. Great leaders treat everyone right, but they don't treat them the same. They realize that one size truly does not fit all. They tap into the uniqueness of each individual to help each one grow to his or her full potential. Outstanding leaders serve with a positive message, and they know how to deliver the tough talk without attacking. When you serve others for the right reasons, they will develop trust in and respect for you.

> "The first responsibility of a leader is to define reality; the last is to say thank you. In between, the leader is a servant."
>
> —Max De Pree, outstanding business leader who wrote Leadership Is an Art and Called to Serve: Creating and Nurturing the Effective Volunteer Board.

The Super Freak Way requires that you always lead with your life, using these seven principles. The chapters in this book will explain each of these principles in more detail with many examples from my life and the lives of other successful leaders.

As a leader, it is important for you to model or demonstrate the behaviors that you would like to see more of in those you lead. While a sermon may sound good, most of us would rather see a sermon demonstrated rather than talked about. Outstanding leadership is a by-product of consistently demonstrating the above seven principles. When we are consistently doing the right thing for the right reasons, excellence is bound to be the end result. Trust and respect are spread throughout the family, school, team, business, or any organization, and winning together is commonplace.

So, as always, my request of you: Please read the following pages with an open mind. Understand that old methods do not equal new results. Read this book with the art of possibilities beating in your heart while starting from ground zero. Stay present in this content and enjoy yourself. My goal for you—after you read *Lead with Your Life*—is that you will become the outstanding leader you were meant to be! Buckle up, hold on, and enjoy another ride on the A-Train!

Chapter 1: People of Character

People of character are individuals who are compelled to do what they say they will do. Having good character plays a key role not only in leadership, but also in the direction of one's career. Though most leaders realize that character is important, many find it hard to come to grips with its content, importance, and meaning. Leaders who lack good character lose opportunities for growth and advancement because they believe they are superior to the people they lead. Though certain individuals on a team may display good character, leaders and teammates may not necessarily recognize these individuals' strength of character. Leaders with character create, display, and promote trust and respect throughout the entire organization, team, business, and/or family. Leaders who trust and respect those they lead inspire individuals to come to work or practice with the right attitudes, behaviors, and efforts.

> "People with good intentions make promises. People with good character keep them."
>
> —*Author unknown*

What does the word "character" mean? In Greek, character translates as "an enduring, or indelible mark." Thus, character might be best defined as "values in action" or the qualities that make up someone's personality or the qualities that clearly make someone different from someone else. Pauline Phillips started the newspaper advice column called "Dear Abby" in 1956. Her daughter, Jeanne Phillips, now writes the column. Abby once wrote these wise words regarding character: "The best index to a person's character is (a) how he or she treats people who can't do him or her any good, and

(b) how he or she treats people who can't fight back." People in leadership positions will confront situations described in both of the above statements. How leaders respond to those who cannot do them any good or who cannot fight back says a whole lot about the leaders' characters.

Our character not only exist in us but also in the minds of others. When we interact with others, no matter how brief or how long the interaction, others make a decision about who we are and what kind of person we are based on that interaction. Therefore, character is a very powerful component in leadership. It is impor-tant because how we see ourselves as leaders might not necessarily be how the people we are leading see us. Perception is reality for each and every one of us. Outstanding leaders more times than not understand this and work diligently to communicate and create a culture that is one of trust and respect for all.

Leaders with character have a cluster of core values that are consistently put into action whether they are relating to a team or to an individual. Great character isn't a result of luck or erratic behavior. We show character when our actions and thoughts are intentionally, freely, logically, and consistently chosen when we compete against other teams or individuals who are said to have character. Character is a collection of related processes, such as displaying honesty, respect, perseverance, and courage, as we solve problems, show our feelings, and interact with others. Other values of character in leadership are humility, collaboration, and going beyond normal expectations. Leaders must demonstrate each one of these values if a team, organization, business, or family are to achieve long-term progress and success.

Leaders who display strong character have a strong sense of respectfulness for others. They think of the needs of the people they are leading and put those needs ahead of their own. When leaders focus on the good of the people, their organization, business, school, or family will thrive. Success at any level is driven by the attitudes, behaviors, and efforts of people, not by products or things. The role of a leader is not to make all of the decisions for each team member; it is to get the people who have access to the right information together, so that collectively, they are able to make better decisions than they would have on their own. Great leaders find the right resources and distribute them throughout the organization to get the desired results. Being respectful to others at all times creates trust between the leader and the team and among team members. With mutual trust, the organization will compete at a high level, be successful, and win more consistently. Without trust and respect between leaders and team members, success at any level will be hard to come by. When leaders and team members trust and respect each other, that is a clear sign of good character throughout the team. And when all members of the team from top to bottom have trust and respect for one another, they will achieve their goals.

A leader who is a person of character also understands the value of getting his or her people to work and play together. Working together for the good of the team is vital if team and personal goals are to be met. It is not always easy to get everyone to cooperate when pursuing a vision, mission, or goal; however, leaders with character can bring people together and win more times than not. These leaders show fairness to every team member, which says, "You are valuable." When you are a person of character, you understand that one size does not fit all. In the words of my grandfather, Wilson Gunter, "Treat everyone right, but don't you dare treat them the same." Successful leaders make a point to get to know all of their people. As a leader, when you connect with your team members in ways that show each person's success is important to you, each one will always work hard for you. They will follow wherever you lead because of the trust and respect created among the leadership and team members.

Leaders with character are compassionate and display wisdom. When you are a compassionate person, you listen to others, and more importantly, you hear and understand them. Compassionate leaders place themselves in the shoes of their people to empathize with what each team member is going through. Compassionate leaders take the necessary steps to understand and act upon the needs and concerns of their people. These leaders display wisdom by drawing upon their experience and knowledge to make the best decisions possible for their people and the organization, business, school or family. Good character is built by learning from doing and then making the necessary adjustments to succeed. People of character share information from past successes or opportunities for improvement to help others make more informed decisions for their lives. When leaders share wisdom, they cut into the learning curve of the members of their team, which helps them make greater progress. Team members will make their own mistakes, yet because their leaders have shared information, they are not likely to make the same mistakes others have made. People of character share informa-tion openly and willingly. They know that sharing information is the key to success.

Good character also takes courage. As a leader, it's not easy to always be up and on top of your game. Leadership at times requires hard talks, hard decisions, and being unpopular, but that is where courage comes in. It's easy to lead with your life when everything is going great, but true character and leadership will always shine through in times of adversity. Adversity reveals who we are, what we are made of, and what we can handle. Courage is what gets us through these moments. No matter who you are, where you grew up, who your parents are, and so on, at some point adversity will show up in your life, and your character will be tested. The end result of that test will be directly proportionate to the courage you display while overcoming the adversity. When we act with courage, we run the risks of not succeeding; however, courage is a necessary ingredient if we are to succeed. When you are a person of character, your courage is not constrained by the fear of the unknown—it actually thrives on the art of possibilities.

"Everyone wants to be a lion . . . until they have to do lion shit!"

—*Andrew Read, endurance, strength, and conditioning coach, Melbourne, Australia.*

Character, like every other thing in life that has stood the test of time, can only last if it is built on a strong foundation. No one can say for certain how much character we develop in our early years; however, it is safe to say that character does not change quickly. A person's behavior could be an indication of that person's character, such as weak, strong, good, or bad. Strong character may be indicated by drive, energy, self-determination, willpower, and a can-do attitude. Several factors shape our character, such as environment, role models, and socio-economic status. These factors shape the moral character in each of us. As we grow, we start to develop concern for others, a sense of justice, and integrity. We become conscious of social pressures and develop problem-solving and leadership skills. These factors also influence how we develop a healthy lifestyle, life goals, self-discipline, and self-control, all of which help us commit to staying the course to achieve our goals.

Leaders with character take responsibility for living the life they want while they inspire others around them. They hold themselves accountable for doing whatever it takes to compete and be successful as individuals and as a team. Leaders with character focus on developing their own knowledge, deepening their understanding of social and mental skills, and staying committed to living out their core values. They have a sense of process, purpose, and structure. They share an interest with team members in building a strong foundation as well as planning for successful outcomes. Another way of saying this is leaders with character work to get the desired results for their team. They have the ability to adapt to any situation to get the desired results. Leaders with character develop their skills through healthy competition. They know they can only achieve their best when they challenge and support each team member. Leaders with character feel as responsible for the growth of their team members as they do for their own development, because it is through the strength of community that we as leaders get the most from ourselves. At every level of competition, participants achieve new levels of excellence when they find good competitors. Leaders with character come to understand that competition is "striving with" instead of "striving against." By coming to this understanding, we appreciate, value, and even seek out competitors who will help get the best out of us. Good examples are Muhammad Ali vs. Joe Frazier, Martina Navratilova vs. Chris Evert, and Larry Bird vs. Magic Johnson.

Building a strong foundation for character is a simple as applying the ABE (Attitude, Behavior, and Effort) principle. Attitude,

Behavior, and Effort are all things that every individual gets to control. Each and every day we get to decide what our attitude will be. I was taught a very long time ago by my grandfather that attitude only came in two flavors: good or bad. There is no in between. Leaders with character focus on maintaining a positive attitude no matter the circumstances, obstacles, or opportunities that lie ahead of them each day. When we wake up every morning, we get to choose what our attitude for the day will be. Behavior, like attitude, comes in only two flavors. We all get to choose to behave well or badly. Most of us know the right things to do, but doing them consistently requires work daily. Conducting ourselves in the appropriate way 24/7 requires 100-percent focus and never taking a play off.

And finally, effort: Leaders with character are always committed to working very hard for the good of the team. Following the ABE (Attitude, Behavior, and Effort) principle will shape our character. These three ingredients together will start the process for building a strong foundation of character. Great leaders and teams cannot win consistently without people of character as leaders and team members. When leaders and team members are people of character, together they will leave a legacy of hope and achievement.

Character matters at every level if an organization, business, team, or family is going to be successful. The more competent we are in our leadership abilities, the more we will do as leaders.

> "As a leader, commitment determines what we want to do, but character determines what we will do."
>
> —Almon W. Gunter, Jr.

If we are going to make effective decisions, we must have character as our foundation. No one is perfect, and at some point we all fall short or fail at something. Often times, the failing that we experience can be linked back to a failing in our character. For example, as leaders when we don't admit that we lack a certain competency to succeed and/or lead, the root issue is character. It takes character to challenge decisions made by others that you feel are wrong. As a leader, when you're not willing to listen to others because you fear they may undermine your leadership, this is a character issue. Leaders with character create a culture in which others can challenge leaders' decisions without fear of consequences. Dealing with the attitudes, behaviors, and efforts of others on a daily basis requires character. These are a few examples of why character matters in leadership.

Warren Bennis addressed the role of individual responsibility in becoming a better leader when he said,

> "The leader never lies to himself, especially about himself, knows his flaws as well as his assets, and deals with them directly. You are your own raw material. When you know what you consist of and what you want to make of it, then you can invent yourself."
>
> —Warren Bennis, a scholar, author, and advisor to presidents and business executives on how to be successful leaders.

Bennis's statement above is as relevant to leaders' characters as much as it is to their competencies and commitment to achieving success. Furthermore, following Bennis's advice requires self-awareness, preparedness, and willingness to examine habitual behaviors. You may decide to consider whether there are better ways of leading than the ones that have worked, more or less, for you in the past. We limit our development as leaders when we do not have the discipline and courage to assess ourselves honestly. We need to look in the mirror and ask ourselves the hard questions. The mirror doesn't lie.

Character is not something that you have or don't have. All of us have character, but the key is the development of each phase of our character so we can lead others effectively. Character is not something that can be turned on and off at will. Every situation presents a different learning experience for you and an opportunity to strengthen your character. In particular, when we face adversity, our character will shine through most clearly. The development of character is a journey that lasts a lifetime. With that in mind, just know that there will be days when we will rise to the occasion and other days when we'll disappoint ourselves and those around us. Competencies count, character matters, and commitment to the leadership role is critical to the leader's success. That is the beauty of life. We constantly get to write our own stories.

Scribbles and Doodles

List three people from history you consider to be great leaders. (List five character traits for each that make him or her a great leader.)

_____
_____
_____
_____
_____
_____
_____
_____
_____
_____

List three people in your, family, industry, organization, or among your friends you consider to be great leaders. (List five character traits for each that make him or her a great leader.)

___

Looking at your above lists, did you learn anything new? (If so, precisely what?)

___

Final Thoughts:

Chapter 2: Visionaries

Outstanding leaders are visionaries. They have a sense of mission and purpose, or, as I like to say, they know what they are playing for. Leaders who have vision work with incredible imaginations, thoughtful insights, and are the builders of bridges for others to cross. They present challenges that call forth the best in people and bring them together around a shared sense of purpose and understanding. They work with the power of intentionality and are driven to fulfill a higher purpose. Visionary leaders' eyes are always on the horizon, not just on what is near at hand. They see the big picture. Outstanding leaders are innovators and agents of change for all. Strategic thinking is one of their major assets. There is a profound connection between the leader and what's best for all; thus, true visionary leaders serve the good of all. No matter the issues, visionaries who are leaders recognize that there is some truth to both sides. They search for solutions that go well beyond the usual adversarial approaches. Instead, they figure out what is causing problems and work with all team members to solve problems. Leaders with vision address the root causes of both sides of an issue and look for ways to create real breakthroughs.

Visionaries may dream wonderful visions of the future and articulate them with great inspiration because they are good with words. However, effective leaders who are visionaries are good with actions as well as words, so they can bring their vision into being in the world to transform it in some way. More than words are needed to make a vision a reality. It requires leadership, focus, discipline, drive, and heartfelt commitment to the vision, mission, and goal of the organization, team, school, or family.

Leaders with vision create specific, achievable goals, initiate action, and enlist the participation of others. They inspire people to be better than they already are. They promote a partnership approach and create a shared sense of vision and meaning with others. They exhibit a great respect for others and carefully develop team spirit and team learning. Leaders with vision anticipate change and are proactive rather than reactive to events. Their focus is on opportunities, not on problems. They emphasize win/win—rather than adversarial win/lose—approaches.

Vision is the source of discipline and the root of leadership. Successful leaders know that one of the keys to life is finding a vision, a great idea that causes them to want to impose discipline upon themselves. To be a great leader you must have self-discipline. Having a vision for your own life and for your organization, team, school, business, or family is critical if you are going to live your life with purpose. When your vision is clear, you will find that your life is simpler. Having a vision simplifies life because it narrows your focus, and in the game of life we achieve what we focus on. Without a clear vision, leaders cannot hit the mark consistently. Vision controls the choices you make for yourself and for your team. As a leader, once you know your vision, you can assess where you are and, more importantly, you will understand which actions will and will not help you and your people achieve the vision. Simply stated, if you know what to do to help you and your team achieve success, you will also know what not to do. The knowledge of knowing what you are playing for will dictate the choices and decisions you make for the organization, team, school, business, family, and yourself.

Nothing is more fulfilling for a leader than having a true sense of mission and purpose.

Leaders who are visionaries see things as they can be. They don't stress over things that may not happen. For each of us, it's important to remember that we do not know everything, and we cannot do everything by ourselves. Visionaries know it will take people working together, each doing what he or she does best, to make any dream come true. When we fear the unknown or when we are forced to move out of our comfort zone, we become stressed. Leaders with vision live for the art of possibilities. It is in the art of possibilities where real progress is made. Success doesn't come from wanting to be successful; success comes from making yourself valuable, which always starts with a thought.

"You're only as good as you believe you are."

—*Almon W. Gunter, Jr.*

Every substantial achievement in life starts as an idea, a vision, a belief. When you find your vision, you will ultimately find your value and voice. And it's your value as a person that people ultimately pay for.

As leaders we need to know the difference between sight and vision. Sight is seeing things as they are, which is how many people live their lives each day. Vision, on the other hand, is seeing things as they can be. Leaders who have vision embrace the unknown instead of fearing it. When others say, "It's never been done before," visionary leaders say, "Let's be the first to do it!" Leaders with vision live, breathe, and work for possibilities. They know that every vision at various points will get tested, and they welcome the challenges, understanding that their vision will be validated as authentic. Great leaders are free from fear of failing. They are more inclined to fear not trying at all or quitting before they even get started. Visionaries know the price they are willing to pay to pursue their vision. They've already answered the question, "What are you willing to give up to achieve the vision, mission, and goal?" Visionary leaders always start with the end result in mind and work backwards from there. They constantly serve their vision, which is invisible to others. Most people believe something only when they see it. Visionaries see a concept for the future in their minds, and then they believe it! Having vision for your life gives you the following benefits: (1) clarifies your purpose, (2) gives you direction, and (3) empowers you beyond your assets. When your vision is clearly defined, you know what you are playing for. Every day you'll give 100-percent effort to your cause because your purpose for being and doing is clear. You have direction and a road map to follow that will lead you to your destiny. With direction and a plan, you have greater flexibility, so detours, missteps, and adversity do not drag you into a tailspin. And finally, vision allows you to think outside the box. Better yet, there is no box; there are only possibilities. You're free to let go and be open to whatever the universe brings your way. More times than not, everything you need will come your way. When your vision is clear, it will always create and attract the resources needed to succeed.

Leaders with vision have a higher expectation of the world than most. They expect more from the world, and they take actions to meet and exceed their expectations. Vision forces you not to think or play small. It demands that you build each day upon the day before. When you have vision, it will force you to have the courage to take risks. Courage tells you: if you risk nothing and do nothing, you get nothing. It takes courage and a boatload of faith to take risks each day, chasing something you may not get. Yet, risks must be taken to produce progress and growth. Leaders with vision have the courage and faith to dare to dream and hope for something beyond themselves. Without vision, we risk living lives filled with resentment and regret. Successful leaders follow their visions with courage and faith until their visions become realities.

When it comes to leadership, vision is a key component to developing the one mission with a one-goal philosophy. This philosophy cannot exist without one vision. A clear vision sets the tone for what each day will be for you. To be successful, you will do what you need to do. There are no shortcuts for achieving success. In other words, your vision makes choices for you. It will decide what your priorities are for each day. You'll set aside enough time each day to accomplish your goals instead of only trying halfheartedly. Your vision will choose your attitude and behavior, as well as your circle of influence each day. Success at any level depends greatly upon who you spend your time with and what you give your time to. When your vision is clear, you will no longer have to worry about choosing your attitude, friends, future, and values for your life. Your vision will choose these things for you. Because you want to be successful your attitude will be good, and you will select friends who are uplifting, inspiring, and supportive to you and your dreams. You will choose to see your future as bright, and you will always set your priorities with a positive end in mind.

When you truly *Lead with Your Life*, you'll realize that having a vision clarifies your purpose. It gives you a reason to work hard and be accountable for doing the work required to achieve your destiny. Vision gives you direction, and with direction you have better opportunities to plan and prepare to achieve your destiny.

With proper planning, you have greater flexibility when adversity shows up at your door. Every dream or destiny will come with a price of adversity, setbacks, and missteps. So having a clear direction is essential for hitting your mark. As a leader with vision, you are empowered beyond your assets. What this means is everything you need to succeed will come when you need it. When you are sure of your purpose and doing what you are supposed to do with your life, your needs will be met, and all of the resources required to win will be at your disposal. Vision frees you from the fear of the unknown and puts you in the realm of operating with the mindset of being open to all possibilities.

Visionaries are risk-takers who embrace the unknown. They have remarkable courage to go after their destiny each and every day with no guarantee of success. Leaders who show this kind of courage walk the talk of faith. They simply trust that all of their needs will be met. Leaders with vision set high expectations for themselves but also for the world as a whole. They expect everything and everyone to play at the maximum level each day. Setting high expectations is a key principle for achieving success. Most people would rather aim low and hit an easy goal than aim high and miss. The reality is leaders with vision know that aiming high is the only way barriers are broken and true progress is made. To produce the most remarkable wins, take the risks, show courage, and live in the state of being uncomfortable.

Leaders with vision are more than dreamers. The dream is where it starts, but then they take action to make their dream a reality. Visionaries create a plan that makes the journey to success doable by starting with a vision that is clear and simple. Leaders with vision know that success at the highest level will always be hard but doesn't need to be complicated. So keeping things clear and simple allows for a greater chance of proper execution. Visionaries also make time to reevaluate their vision and monitor the progress made. Success is achieved more consistently when you know where you are on your journey. Without a strong foundation and infrastructure, nothing substantial will stand over a long period of time. Visionaries put their dreams and desires on paper to hold themselves accountable for going after what they want. It takes courage to write your dreams and even more courage to share them with others. However, leaders with vision share their vision in the hopes that others will be inspired and join in on the journey. Success at any level will always take dreaming, planning, and working the plan. *Visionaries Dream It. Dare It. Do It.*

Scribbles and Doodles

What is your vision for the next five years of your life? (personally and professionally)

_____
_____
_____
_____
_____
_____
_____
_____
_____
_____

Based on your vision, what choices have you made in order to succeed?

_____
_____
_____
_____
_____
_____
_____
_____
_____
_____
_____
_____
_____
_____

List five components of a clear and simple vision.

_____
_____
_____
_____
_____
_____
_____
_____
_____
_____
_____

Final Thoughts:

Chapter 3: Communicating the Vision

Outstanding leaders communicate their vision with optimism and hope to every member of the team. Great leaders are salespersons of the art of possibilities. Outstanding leaders know the right words to speak to their team not only at the right times but every time. More importantly, exceptional leaders let their actions inspire others by walking the talk. Their actions and words constantly paint a picture that everyone within the organization can see and embrace as their own. Great leaders model the way for others to follow each day.

> "People need to see a vision to connect with it, which is why the great communicators harness imagery to amplify the power of their message. Storytelling gets much more mileage than fact-spewing. However, the best representation of a vision occurs when a leader embodies it. People sooner follow what they see than what they hear. When a leader is ablaze with passion, people invariably are attracted to the flame."
>
> —John C. Maxwell, author, speaker, pastor, and coach, author of The 21 Indispensable Qualities of a Leader: Becoming the Person Others Will Want to Follow

As a leader with an incredible vision, if you do not have the ability to communicate your vision to the rest of the organization, it is all for nothing. You need to develop the ability to communicate so that every member on the team buys in to your vision. This is critical. As a leader you know that to get to the top, there will be adversity and obstacles along the way, so the ability to communicate your message with optimism and hope is necessary to keep the team moving in the right direction. You must have the ability to stop any negative talk among team members. When adversity rears its head and things are not on track, it is easy for team members to turn negative and lose sight of the vision. As a visionary leader, you must stop the negative behavior and attitude in team members dead in their tracks. One of the ways to squash the negative talk is to reassure your team that reaching the vision, mission, and goal of the organization can and will be obtained—only by working together as a team and maximizing individuals' efforts each day.

Leading with your life starts and ends with effective communication. As a leader, when you connect with individuals, it means you have found a way to relate and identify with your team members, which allows you to have influence over their actions. Leaders who connect with their team members know that the best connections are made when you can show all team members (1) that you care for them, (2) that you can help them reach their goal/s, and (3) that they can trust you to do what you say you will do. Once these three things are established, the leader then gains the respect of team members. Successful leaders know how to connect with their team; they must focus on not only what they say, but how they say it, as well as what they look like when they say it (body language). All of these factors matter if your vision is to be communicated effectively. And truth be told, how you say things and what you look like when you speak (body language) is more important than the words that you choose to speak. Effectively communicating your vision ultimately boils down to your energy and passion for your vision.

To communicate effectively as a leader, you must display several things to your team in order for each team member to buy into the vision. First, to deliver a message that will inspire them, you must be prepared. Preparation allows for greater flexibility in the things that you are saying and doing. When you are prepared, you have a far greater chance of being successful and achieving your desired results. When a leader is unprepared, he or she sends the wrong message to the team. Second, as a leader you must be committed to your vision, your message, and your team. When team members know that their leader is all in, it is much easier as a team member to buy into the vision, mission, and goals of the team. Third, as a leader you must be interested in the people you lead, the work you are doing, and why you are doing it. Fourth, you need the ability to be comfortable being uncomfortable. You embrace adversity. Challenges are viewed as opportunities instead of as roadblocks. You live each day as your authentic self. The bottom line: to be effective when it comes to communicating in a way that you hit your mark as a leader, you must be prepared, committed, and interesting, and you must feel comfortable being uncomfortable.

Your vision as a leader is best communicated when you focus on solutions. Optimism and hope are communicated and accepted when you search for ways to win versus focusing on negatives or blaming others for why things are not working. By actively problem-solving together as a leader with your team members, you actually feel as though you are regaining control of your situation. When you feel as though you are in control, you start to regain confidence and find better ways to reframe the adversity or obstacles that you face. Leaders who communicate a clear vision know how to reframe obstacles as opportunities. They communicate resilience and hope during difficult moments, which gives the rest of the team greater opportunities to respond favorably. When you lead from the front, you always communicate a solution-driven message that consists of hope and optimism.

Leaders who communicate a clear vision do so by making sure that they are realistic in what it will take as a team to win, the resources needed to win, and the commitment that will need to be made by all to succeed as a team. In other words, they make the impossible possible by putting their vision into manageable resources, skills, and timeframes. Great leaders know that failure along the way will happen, but they communicate the message that failure is a part of the overall success process. The lessons learned through failure often provide the critical pieces needed to succeed. Failure should never be considered fatal. When failure is looked upon with solution-driven eyes, the outcome is usually a fresh approach and a win in the end. Though successful leaders always communicate hope and optimism, they also communicate real threats when they occur. Being optimistic or hopeful doesn't and shouldn't mean denying reality. Great leaders always keep it real and gain the trust and respect of their greatest driving force—their people!

When you *Lead with Your Life*, you have the opportunity to inspire others daily. There is a major difference between inspiring versus motivating individuals. It is my belief that individuals are inspired to do great things instead of being motivated to do great things. My philosophy is you cannot motivate individuals to do something or be something that they do not want to be. As a parent, teacher, mentor, or leader, how many times have you given an individual the right information, at the right time, for the right reason, to do the right thing to succeed, and he or she did not make the right decision? Not only did the person not make the right decision the first time, but you repeated the information a second, third, and fourth time, and he or she still did not make the right decision. If there was such a thing as motivation, he or she would have taking the information and done the right thing the first time or certainly the second time, right?! After all, how could someone not want to be successful, especially when you are giving them the information they need to do so?

As the parent, teacher, mentor, or leader, you're probably saying to yourself, "I know what I'm talking about, I've experienced a few things, I know how this will play out, so you have to listen to me!" Then you question yourself: Why can't I motivate him or her?! Well, because you can't motivate an individual to do or be something that he or she is not ready to do or be.

My grandfather, Wilson Gunter, used to say, "You will do or be what you want to do or be when it becomes important to you. And not one second before that." My philosophy is that people don't look to be motivated—they look to be inspired. When people are inspired, there is no need to worry about motivation. They will become self-motivated, self-disciplined, and begin to write their own story of success. Motivation is a byproduct of inspiration. When you lead from your life, you utilize the art of storytelling to communicate your vision. Utilizing powerful stories is a great way to make connections with your team. Providing information through stories helps shape the perspective of your vision and brings your vision into focus for your team. People commit to being great when failure is not an option and when the consequences for not succeeding become more painful than their consciences can stand. Storytelling provides this kind of inspiration for individuals. It provides a reference point or benchmark that makes us believe and see that the possibility for greatness is within our reach. Every extraordinary thing that has been achieved was first conceived by an ordinary person having a vision. When our vision is communicated clearly and concisely, the impossible becomes possible.

Great leaders never stop inspiring. They constantly put themselves out front not to say, hey look at me, but to create and clear a path for each team member to succeed. Successful leaders always lead from the front with their own lives, and they never leave their team guessing about the direction in which they are going. Outstanding leadership requires that the leader is a great verbal communicator. But the ability to communicate verbally isn't where it stops; great leaders walk their talk and practice what they preach. They know that succeeding will come with greater consistency when team members see leaders doing what they ask of the team instead of just talking about it. I often say, "The world is full of big talkers and little walkers." It is so easy to talk a good game, but winning at any level at some point will always require action.

When you *Lead with Your Life*, you realize that connecting with the people you are leading is more about the skill of doing certain things right versus having a natural talent. Natural talent will only get you so far. To be a great leader, your core foundation is made of the skills you have developed along the way. Great leaders know that having a vision is essential, but the key to the overall success of the vision depends on knowing how to make people want to listen to you. Having something important to say is great, but to move the idea forward, the people you lead must be willing to listen to you and actually hear what you are saying and take action based on what you are saying.

Great leaders draw on five main factors when communicating their vision to connect with and inspire people to listen to the vision. They draw on the following strengths:

- **Relationships.** What they've learned from the people who have mentored, challenged, and helped them in their own growth.

- **Sacrifices.** How they have chosen to live to obtain their goals over time.
- **Insights.** What they know that can benefit others in the long run, including bridges they have built that can save those they lead from certain pitfalls.
- **Successes.** What they have accomplished through trial and error, their abilities to outlast the setbacks and do whatever it takes to succeed.
- **Abilities.** What they can do, the tools and skills that they possess to make them qualified to lead.

These five factors help successful leaders win attention of their people to be inspired by them.

Leaders who communicate their vision in an effective way do so because they don't focus on themselves. They work hard to seek out common ground everyone can relate to and buy into. When you *Lead with Your Life*, you are always searching for a win-win for everyone.

Successful leaders stay away from the following traps:
- **Feeling Indifference.** Not caring about what others want, feel, or know.
- Making **Assumptions.** Thinking they already know what their people want, feel, and know.
- **Arrogance.** Communicating and acting in ways that show they believe they're more important than those they lead. Not caring about others' ideas.
- **Control.** Asserting their own will over others to maintain dominance over them, often by instilling fear in others.

Leaders who connect with their people at the highest level never fall prey to these four traps or pitfalls. Great verbal communicators work continuously to maintain the right connections with their people so all understand their vision clearly.

Scribbles and Doodles

List three ways in which you communicate optimism and hope to your family, friends, colleagues, and acquaintances.

___

List five ways you show your family, friends, or colleagues that you care about them, that you can help them reach their goal(s), and that they can trust you.

___

When you communicate your vision, how do you get people to want to hear what you have to say?

Final Thoughts:

Chapter 4: Competencies

Outstanding leaders are competent in their abilities to lead their teams to success. Being competent is knowing the job and knowing what it takes to maximize the potential of everyone on the team. Competent leaders don't claim to have all of the answers; however, they utilize every resource available to them to make sure that each member on the team has what he or she needs to be successful. They do what they say they will do, which creates trust and respect among leadership and the worker bees. Competent leaders aren't afraid to make mistakes. They hold themselves to the same high standards as they hold each team member. Outstanding leaders, through consistency, communication, and follow-up, create an environment of trust and respect throughout the organization.

> "The secret joy in work is . . . excellence. To know how to do something well is to enjoy it."
> —Pearl S. Buck, American novelist who won the Pulitzer Prize for her book *The Good Earth*.

To be a competent leader, you must be willing to work hard to develop leadership skills that will allow you to lead from the front. Successful leaders realize to be effective they must have certain skills that create a winning environment, workplace, or team that people want to be a part of. To create such an environment, successful leaders start with the skill of being passionate. Passion says that you personally are sold on the work you are doing. It sends the message to the staff that the work that is being done is important to both internal and external customers. *In this book, we make a distinction between internal and external customers.* Internal customers are the people you employ. They are the team members that look to you for your guidance each day to be the best version of themselves. External customers are your clients, the people who depend on your products or services to achieve their goals or vision.

The enthusiasm of the leader goes a long way toward building employee confidence, trust, and respect. Passion fosters positive employee morale, which leads to greater productivity throughout the organization. Developing the skill of passion is done by knowing your vision, understanding why you are committed to it, and taking the risk to see it through to the end. Successful leaders work to develop contagious enthusiasm throughout the organization, which contributes greatly to their overall competence.

Competent leaders know how to communicate the vision, goals, and mission of the organization. Developing the skills to be a great communicator starts with being a good listener. Listening is a skill that is often overlooked when it comes to being competent in what you do. Listening is the key to collecting information to develop the message that needs to be delivered right. To deliver the right message, leaders need to make sure they first have the right information. Information is gained through listening. You only grow through gaining information, so the more you listen to your team members, the more information you gain. The more information you gain, the more you grow. Competence at the highest levels starts with being a good listener.

Leaders who are considered great communicators of vision, goals, and mission are also masters of presentation. They work diligently on developing the skill of being able to present information in a timely, decisive manner. They utilize every resource they have to make sure they are providing their people with the resources they need to have the best chance of hitting and exceeding their goals. Successful, competent leadership requires a commitment to passion, communication, and presentation.

Competent leaders also focus on the skill of building a team. They concentrate on surrounding themselves with people of character and people who are focused, disciplined, and driven to excellence. Assembling team members who are committed to the vision, goals, and mission of the organization is no easy task. It requires a leader who is confident and competent in his or her abilities to make the right connections at the right time, as well as know how to recognize and identify the right talent for the team. Building a great team, maintaining a great team, and inspiring a great team to play hard every day is a tough task for any leader. Successful leaders constantly work toward providing tools that will benefit the entire team in the pursuit of vision, mission, and goal(s). A winning team requires putting together a group of people who live daily these principles that are essential for creating the essence of teamwork. All team members live out the following:

- People of Character
- Outstanding Leadership Skills
- Trust and Respect for All Team Members
- Outstanding Talent
- Commitment
- Passion
- Empowerment of Other Team Members
- The Ability to Think Team

Competent leaders must develop and utilize the skill of self-awareness. As a leader it is important that you never stop learning.

Great leaders know that they do not know it all, so they are eager to learn through additional training, being mentored, or by reading and researching. They are aware that the people they are entrusted to lead are only as good as the information that they are receiving from the leader. Success or opportunities for improvements will always be directly related to the information received and the decisions that are made utilizing that information—no matter who you are, where you live, where you are from, or any other variable. Competent leaders are open to feedback from everyone because they are focused on receiving a well-rounded review of their job performance as leaders. Competent individuals strive to be the best version of themselves. The skill of self-awareness leads to a greater understanding of self-worth and self-growth.

Competent leaders also strive to develop the skill of knowing how to delegate responsibilities effectively. As a leader, it is critical that you understand that doing the work for others or not letting go of details that can be delegated will lead to your isolation and ineffectiveness and make you appear to be insecure as a leader. You cannot develop future leaders by doing things for your people that they should be doing for themselves. Competent leaders know that taking on all the work of the organization and not delegating to others will only lead to a disastrous outcome.

A leader's proper delegation empowers team members and creates a stronger bond within the entire team. When we empower others, we let go and send a clear message that we believe in the individual. Empowerment says we trust, respect, and know that others can get it done. As a leader, letting go so others can achieve is the ultimate compliment. Effective delegation will also require that you and your team members are resilient. Every organization, no matter what the product or service is, will come under attack by stress, uncertainty, and setbacks. As a leader, how well you handle these adverse situations will speak volumes to how well your team will handle them. *Ultimately, as a leader, your actions will say more to your team than any speech you can give.* Your ability as a leader to bounce back, stay focused, and execute after a setback is key to creating the winning environment you want for your team and organization.

There are several other skills that a competent leader must have in his or her tool belt in order to lead from the front:

- Shows Integrity and Honesty
- Has the Abilities to Solve Problems and Analyze Issues
- Inspires His or Her Team.

Integrity and honesty are key components for any great leader. The best way to gain trust and respect from the people you lead is to do what you say you will do. Leaders who walk the talk, show respect for their people, and create an environment that is built for others to learn, risk, and grow will always be successful. People want to work for good people. They want leaders they can trust: leaders who say the right things for the right reasons. But more important, people want leaders who do the right thing. As a leader, your actions will always model the way for your people. Teams ultimately succeed or fall short based on the actions of the leader. Morale is always a direct reflection of the actions of the leadership. One sure way as a competent leader to win more consistently is to be honest and display integrity to your followers as well as yourself.

Being competent as a leader also requires *the ability to solve problems and analyze issues.* After all, in the game of life, ultimately you are rewarded financially for the problems you solve. In other words, if you find a problem, you just found your business! Leaders who are solution driven will always achieve greater success. When you lead with your life, one of your main objectives should be finding solutions. Everyone loves a winner. So when you are solving problems and analyzing issues and coming up with solutions that work, your people will follow your lead, and the outcome 9 out of 10 times will be favorable. Leaders who can assess a situation and then provide the resources for a positive solution will always gain the trust and respect of their teams.

No leader can build and sustain a winning organization without having *the ability to inspire his or her team*. There is a major difference between inspiration and motivation. People cannot be motivated by other people; they can only be inspired. Motivation is an internal skill—an inside job. Motivation is a choice that can only be made by the individual. As a leader, you should set your sights on inspiring your team. One sure-fire way to inspire others is the art of storytelling. Successful leaders are masters when it comes to storytelling. The right story told at the right time can inspire an entire nation into doing the right thing. When a story is told in a way that connects with individuals, the result is inspiration that leads to self-motivation. Stories can paint pictures that make it easy for individuals to see the big picture of the organization, and they can help individuals visualize their own pictures. People are inspired to be all-in when they know what is in it for them. There is no greater life than a life lived with purpose.

Leaders who are competent in their abilities have a greater chance of inspiring their teams to be greater than they ever thought they could be. The passion of the leaders and how they communicate that passion to the team are critical for the success of the team. Presentation is everything. The words we speak as leaders can elevate the team to incredible heights or deflate and send the team into a downward spiral out of control. Positive communication usually brings about positive growth. The skills of self-awareness, self-worth, and self-growth on the leaders' part will go a long way toward influencing the members of the team. People are inspired more by the things you do versus the things you say. Competent leaders are out front modeling the way for others to follow. In their own lives, leaders set this example: *There are no shortcuts to achieving success. Success will always come at the price of maintaining honesty and integrity day in and day out.*

No team wins consistently without trust and respect throughout the organization from top to bottom and bottom to top. The foundation of trust and respect throughout the organization begins with the honesty and integrity of the leader. His or her actions in these two areas will set the course of organization. Competent leaders are solution driven at all costs. They focus on being problem solvers to keep the team moving forward in a positive direction. Success comes more frequently to teams whose leaders know how to analyze issues and come up with viable solutions that lead to the teams' growth and overall success. Ultimately, to succeed personally and professionally requires the power of inspiration. Successful leaders inspire through stories that touch the very core of their teams. Storytelling can take a flicker of hope and turn it into a raging fire. Competent leaders through it all never stop learning, risking, and growing. They set their hearts, souls, and minds on simply being the very best versions of themselves. And with that kind of mindset, *Everyone Wins!*

Scribbles and Doodles

List three ways in which you communicate passion. (To your family, friends, colleagues, and others)

_____
_____
_____
_____
_____
_____
_____
_____
_____
_____
_____
_____
_____
_____
_____

How do you walk the talk when it comes to honesty and integrity with your family, friends, colleagues, and others?

_____
_____
_____
_____
_____
_____
_____
_____
_____

List five ways in which you delegate or empower others to live out the best versions of themselves (family, friends, colleagues, and others).

_____
_____
_____
_____
_____
_____
_____
_____
_____
_____

Final Thoughts:
_____
_____
_____
_____
_____
_____
_____
_____
_____
_____
_____
_____
_____

Chapter 5: People Skills

Successful leaders uplift, support, and encourage each member of the team every step of the way. Leaders work hard each day to show every member on the team that he or she matters for the success of the team. Great leaders cheer and celebrate the things that they want to see more of within the team. A great example of this type of encouragement can be found in the flight of geese. Geese fly in a V-shaped pattern, and one side of the V is slightly longer than the other. This formation allows the geese to fly more efficiently. The goal of the lead geese is to fly for as long as they can. The honking sound that you hear when geese are in flight is made to encourage and cheer on the lead geese. Great leaders work to create an environment that reflects the flight of the geese mentality.

No one achieves greatness by himself or herself. We all need to be encouraged and picked up when we fall along the way. Great leaders and great teams have the abilities to let go and let all members execute their roles for the good of the team. Outstanding leaders possess the faith needed to go far beyond normal expectations for the possibility of their team becoming a champion.

> "Skill at helping people grow mentally, physically, spiritually, economically, socially, etcetera, like skill at playing chess, depends on understanding and valuing differences."
>
> —*John Ortberg, pastor and motivational speaker who believes "God cares more about who we are becoming than what we do."*

When you *Lead with Your Life*, one of your keys for success will be people skills. People skills are often defined as the ability to listen, to communicate, and to relate to others on a personal or professional level. People skills can also include the ability to work with others toward achieving a common goal, the ability to show empathy, and having the ability to find solutions to problems.

Communication can make or break any relationship. Oftentimes the breakdown in communication is not about what was said, but how it was said. *To communicate effectively as a leader, you must first start with being a good listener.* To be a good active listener, you must work to develop the skills. One way to develop your active listening skills is to focus on the words that the person is saying when he or she is speaking to you. Stay in the present moment, and don't start to formulate what you want to say in response before the other person is finished speaking. Focus completely on what the person is saying, and then repeat the information back in your own words to make sure you understood his or her message.

Think about the times you have been engaged in a hard or confrontational conversation: Are you really listening to what the other person is saying, or are you waiting for them to stop speaking so you can say what you have formulated in your mind? Chances are you didn't hear a word the person said. To communicate effectively, you must be able to take in information, clarify the information, and engage in an effective verbal or written exchange. The only way to make this happen consistently so everyone has a greater chance of being successful is to listen well. Developing your listening skills will allow you to hear what is actually being said, which will give you a greater chance of choosing your words wisely, clarifying the statements the other person is making, and verifying the information you are receiving from that person before responding. The people skill of effective communication, based on active listening and truly understanding others, is priceless in personal and professional relationships.

Successful leaders have a firm grasp of the people skill of empathy as well. They understand how important it is to have the ability to relate to what people are going through. Leaders with empathy have developed the skill of being able to put themselves in others' shoes. Empathy allows you to recognize the thoughts, emotions, and experiences that a person may be going through in the times of crisis or success. The skill of empathy allows a leader to give more personal levels of attention and care and to provide a sympathetic ear if the moment requires it. Empathy is a huge skill for leaders. This skill when developed properly keeps the lines of effective communication open. It creates an environment where the leader is both visible and available to each and every team member. A true open door policy not only says you care but shows that you care.

When you *Lead with Your Life*, another people skill that is a must-have is the skill of patience. Patience is such a tough skill to develop and master. In a world where the norm is to hurry up, multitask, stay busy, and always move, and at the end of the day feel like you are still behind, you must *develop the skill of knowing how to slow down to go fast*. Successful people always move with a purpose. They perfect processes and systems that allow them to stop time so they can do more. My mother, Eunice M. Gunter, would often say, "Learn how to be still. Being still and doing nothing are two totally different things." The older I get, the more sense that statement makes. When you develop patience, you learn to stay even tempered. You have the ability to repeat information accurately to someone who is upset in the most trying situations without losing your cool. Patience is getting to that place where you understand that the light bulb goes on for people at different times. Not everyone will necessarily see what you want them to see when you want them to see it. This is where communication, empathy, and persistence are vital to achieving success as a team.

As a leader, *conflict resolution is a people skill that must be in your tool belt.* Successful leaders know how to mediate disputes and resolve conflicts among internal and external customers. The skill of conflict resolution involves having the ability to clarify a specific dispute, listen to both sides of an argument in a nonjudgmental way, and offer suggestions that will lead to an equitable compromise for all the parties involved. Once again, the people skill of listening and communicating will play key roles in how the conflict will be resolved. The development of the skill of conflict resolution is valuable in creating peace in the workplace, diffusing inner office conflicts, and maintaining a higher overall satisfaction in customer care. Successful leaders know that conflict, challenge, and change will occur in and out of the workplace, and they embrace these things because with conflict, challenge, and change come opportunity, growth, and resolution. It takes pain to bring about change in behavior.

The people skills of respect and tolerance for others are also key components that need to be developed to be a successful leader. Self-respect lays the foundation for your ability to respect others. How we see and act toward ourselves is ultimately how we see and act toward others. My mother, Eunice M. Gunter, also said, "You cannot give what you do not have." As a person you must focus on discovering and developing your value. It is only when you know your own value that you will find your voice.

"Respect is not imposed nor begged; it is earned and offered."

—Almon W. Gunter, Jr.

Your self-concept, self-worth, self-esteem, and self-confidence determine your value, and how you value yourself ultimately determines your voice. Great leaders know how to be the voice for those who cannot speak for themselves, and they know how to build bridges for others to cross.

As a leader, you must develop *the skill of tolerance*. In each of our personal and professional lives, we come into contact with people from every different walk of life. Our socioeconomic backgrounds, culture, ethnicity, religion (and the list goes on) vary, but in the end we are more alike than different. Tolerant people have the ability to accept differences even when they don't agree with them or condone them personally. Leaders with tolerance accept and create an environment where it is all right to agree to disagree. The people skill of tolerance is extremely important for the success of any business, organization, or family because in life one size truly does not fit all.

To improve your overall people skills, consider the following steps. Communication is the cornerstone to having success when it comes to your overall people skills. To communicate effectively, start by actively listening. Show interest in the message that your internal and external customers or team members are communicating by providing affirmations when appropriate, nodding your head, saying, "Okay," or "I understand." Summarize his or her statements and repeat them back to show you are engaged. You are listening, and you are hearing and understanding what is being said.

To develop any skill, you have to be willing to practice. So practice being empathetic to others. Truly work to try to see things from the other person's point of view. When you can communicate that you understand from physical, mental, and emotional standpoints, you will develop trust and respect for each other and build a positive relationship.

Work on being *approachable*. Smile not only with your mouth but with your whole face. A smile goes a long way in creating an environment where everyone feels welcome. Your people want to know that you are approachable and that their opinions matter to you. So be willing to recognize the validity and opinions of each team member. Tolerance and patience are both achieved when you are open and welcome the opinion of others. By working hard to develop these two skills, you may find that your own growth will be enhanced because of the additional input of others. Great leaders surround themselves with the best people. They are always open to the possibilities of what each team member brings to the team.

And a very important point—when working to develop your people skills, *don't take yourself too seriously*. Learn to laugh at yourself and find humor in some of the mistakes that you will make along the way. The ability to admit when you're wrong builds trust and further demonstrates that you are not a leader with a know-it-all mentality. Successful leaders maintain approachability. They work hard each day to create an environment where everyone knows that his or her voice will not only be heard, but will be welcome in every discussion.

To *Lead with Your Life*, you must connect with your business's, organization's, team's, or family's greatest resource, its people! In every business, organization, team, or family, first and foremost, people want to know that they matter. We all have a bit of that "What's in it for me?" (WIIFM) syndrome. Great leaders care for their people professionally and personally. They take a genuine interest in what is really going on in the lives of the people they are leading.

"People don't care what you know until they know that you care."
—Zig Ziglar, author and motivational speaker.

Scribbles and Doodles

As a leader, list five people skills you need to develop in order to lead more effectively. (with family, friends, colleagues, and others)

_____
_____
_____
_____
_____
_____
_____
_____
_____

What do you do each day to make yourself a more effective communicator? (with family, friends, colleagues, and others)

_____
_____
_____
_____
_____
_____
_____
_____
_____

List five ways you show tolerance and patience. (toward family, friends, colleagues, and others)

Final Thoughts:

Chapter 6: Bold Behaviors

When you think of great leaders, it is hard not to associate the word "bold" as one of their many characteristics that help them to lead with their lives. *Merriam-Webster's Dictionary* defines bold in three parts: "not afraid of danger or difficult situations; showing or needing confidence or lack of fear; very confident in a way that may seem rude or foolish." When you consider your list of leaders, one of these definitions most likely applies to each person.

Leaders who are bold and see no obstacles only see opportunities. Bold leaders are very passionate and do not spend time worrying about how they will look in front of others. They are so focused on the goal that sometimes they can appear as though they are foolish in their pursuit of achieving the goal. To lead from the front with your life, you must be confident in your vision, your abilities, and your expertise in helping others share your vision and commitment to achieving it. Boldness requires complete dedication to your purpose and a relentless pursuit of excellence.

> "Boldness does not mean rude, obnoxious, loud, or disrespectful. Being bold is being firm, sure, confident, fearless, daring, strong, resilient, and not easily intimidated. It means you are willing to go where you've never been, willing to try what you have never tried, and willing to trust what you have never trusted. Boldness is quiet, not noisy."
>
> —Mike Yaconelli, writer, church leader, and satirist.

More times than not, the greater the risk, the greater the reward. Bold leaders are not afraid to speak up and to take a risk on developing new products or new personnel. Great leaders take on controversial topics and will sometimes take a position that is contrary to positions of those who are higher up on a particular topic or situation. Bold leaders take personal responsibility for the decisions they make, and typically they are more decisive in making decisions and move at a faster pace than others toward the goal. To lead with your life, you must be willing to think unconventionally, which means sometimes you invest in unproven ideas. Bold leaders set personal and professional goals that are extremely high, they are comfortable making unpopular decisions, and they seek feedback from others. Being bold as a leader shows that you are driven for positive results and innovative in your thinking.

Being bold is like any other skill; the more you work to develop the skill, the better you will become at it. As a leader, not every idea you conceive or decision you make will be popular with your entire team. Anytime you set out to bring about change, some people will sit on the outside looking in. They won't commit fully to the idea, or they will push back regarding the change. As a leader, don't ignore these individuals. This is where your people skills need to kick in and work to help them change their perspectives. Engage them in the process, and keep them close so you have a better opportunity of winning them over to be a part of the bigger picture. Frequently, this is just a matter of communication and presentation. Remember, often it is not what you say but how you say it, and it is not what you do but how you do it. So focus on converting the doubters to believers, and they will become the biggest champions of your cause.

As a leader, taking risks comes with the territory. Bold leaders embrace the notion of risk taking and understand that there is no way you can avoid taking risks if you truly want to learn and grow. Successful leaders learn the right way to take risks. They review all of the factors that are associated with any given risk, and after carefully reviewing these factors, they proceed with either taking the risk or not. Before taking a step forward, successful leaders know that it is critical that they thoroughly assess the risk of any decision. This knowledge allows the leader to have a plan in place in case the risk doesn't pan out or go according to plan. No matter how much you prepare or plan, mistakes happen, and things go wrong, so bold leaders do their best to be ready to weather any storm.

Bold leaders have no tolerance for complacency. Resting on yesterday's laurels is a sure way for an organization to lose its internal and external customers. Bold leaders stay fired up and never lose their spark; therefore, their enthusiasm carries over to their teams. Inertia will never help anyone to grow and maximize his or her potential in the game of life. As a leader, if you want others to champion your cause, you must first be a champion for your own cause. Ultimately, individuals model the behaviors that they see. So as a leader, always celebrate the attitudes, behaviors, and efforts you want to see within the organization.

For many people, being a leader is an uncomfortable position, but when you work to develop the skills needed to lead, it is the best seat in the house. Bold leaders have a cause to fight for. They identify what they believe in, and they hold true to it. This is not an easy position to be in because often this means you may be the only one in the room who thinks that the idea is possible. But this belief, this willingness to hold tight to the idea, to fight to bring your belief to reality is where eventually your boldness will find its cause. You will never commit to fight the good fight until you have something to fight for. You must first believe in something to discover your level of commitment.

Expressing an opinion about things big and small can be another skill that many people feel uncomfortable showing. But again, whatever you want to get better at you must develop through practice. For some, having an opinion can be looked at as a negative thing, but to be bold you can't shy away from having and expressing an opinion. For some, fear may be the reason for not sharing their opinions even when asked by others: fear of being laughed at, fear that no one will agree with them, fear of appearing the fool, whatever the fear may be. To *Lead with Your Life*, you must conquer your fears, find your voice, and express your opinions.

This skill can be developed by saying things as simple as having an opinion about the weather, a color of a couch, or an article of clothing. Get comfortable with people disagreeing with you. Be conscious of your fears, and don't aim to please everyone. If you know what you say is true and legitimate, go for it. When you combine a strong belief in a goal with the ability to handle people disagreeing with you, you will become a bold leader who will become a strong force of nature.

Through hard work and self discovery, bold leaders usually become good speakers. They know how to communicate their vision so that people not only hear it, but they actually see it. People believe what they can see, so painting a picture that allows each team member to see his or her value goes a long way. Leaders who lead with their lives create a winning environment. A winning environment is positive, is built on a can-do attitude, and is centered around "We" instead of "Me." In other words, everyone thinks team first.

This environment energizes the team and makes each individual want to take on the challenges of exceeding professional and personal goals. It pushes the team to a place where all individuals achieve way more than they ever thought possible. There are no undefeated individuals, but there are undefeated teams. No one wins alone. Bold leaders create an environment where continual improvement is the standard, and that standard is challenged every day by each individual on the team. The end goal is for everyone to maximize his or her potential. Individuals will become the best versions of themselves. Bold leaders strive to bring out the very best in everyone.

Everyone has leadership abilities. More importantly, everyone will come to a moment when he or she will lead, follow, or get out of the way. Successful leaders are built over time through trial and error. Leaders do not become bold because they were born that way. They become bold because they put in the time developing the mindset and the skills necessary to fulfill their mission. We are our own worst critics. We beat ourselves up and take the path of least resistance. For many of us, it is simply easier to think that leaders are born versus developed. However, I believe you become what you work to become.

Bold leaders put in the time working to develop the skills that will position them at the front of the line. Here are examples of important skills for bold leaders:

They let their work speak for them. It's a lot easier to get individuals to listen when you come in with a winning track record. Accomplishments create credibility.

They know the risks and prepare to minimize them. Great leaders do not make bold statements or bold moves without knowing the risks and evaluating the cost of the risks for the organization and its people. Great leaders always look for the best plan for success, starting with risks versus rewards.

Your vision is important; fight for it. Bold leaders fight for what they believe. They do not back down. If standing alone until others buy in is what it takes, they gladly do so. Bold leaders are all-in all of the time when it comes to what they believe.

Get buy-in from your front-line people. If you are going to make bold moves, change is going to occur. In the business world, that means the management team and the people on the front line must have a chance to express their views about the change. It is important that the front-line people know their value and the importance that they bring to the team. Without buy-in from the people who actually do the work, change will be slow and painful.

Know your customers and talk their talk. To move forward and do things that have never been done before, your internal and external customers must be on board. So communicate your plan using language that is familiar to them. This is where excellent people skills really pay dividends.

Develop change agents at the executive level. If you are going to be bold, the executive team has to be champions for change as well. For an organization to grow to be all that it can be requires that change occurs across the entire organization. Remember people model the attitudes, behaviors, and efforts they see.

When you consider current or historical great leaders, you will find that they all have one thing in common—they are risks takers. Each person was willing to dare to be different. They were bold in statements and in actions. They were more than visionaries; they were communicators and builders of the most important asset of all—people.

Scribbles and Doodles

As a leader, list three statements or actions you have taken in the past three months that you would consider to be bold (in the presence of family, friends, colleagues, and others).

_____
_____
_____
_____
_____
_____
_____
_____
_____
_____
_____

What fear (if any) has stopped you from making bold statements or taking bold steps toward what you believe? (Please explain.)

_____
_____
_____
_____
_____
_____
_____
_____
_____
_____

List five skills that you will work on in the next three months that will make you a bolder leader.

Final Thoughts:

Chapter 7: Servant Leaders

Of all the principles that great leaders possess, none is greater than the principle of being a servant of the people and for the people. When you *Lead with Your Life*, you are a servant of men and women every day. Your goal is to provide the resources needed for each team member to achieve his or her maximum potential personally and professionally. As a servant leader, you will find that truer words have never been spoken than these: "It's better to give than to receive." And, "It's impossible to help others without helping yourself." Great leaders understand these two concepts better than most, and that's why they succeed.

Serving others is not always easy to do, but in order to lead with your life consistently, it's the right thing to do. The real beauty of voluntary servitude is that each of us can do it. It doesn't require anything more than having a heart to serve and a love for helping people to become the best versions of themselves. In other words, love for people must be in your soul.

> "The servant-leader is a servant first.... Becoming a servant-leader begins with the natural feeling that one wants to serve, to serve first. Then conscious choice brings one to aspire to lead. That person is sharply different from one who is a leader first.... The difference manifests itself in the care taken by the servant first to make sure that other people's highest priority needs are being served. The best test, and the most difficult to administer, is this: Do those served grow as persons? Do they, while being served, become healthier, wiser, freer, more autonomous, more likely themselves to become servants?"
>
> —*Robert K. Greenleaf, originator of the concept of servant leadership, from his essay,* "The Servant as Leader," in Servant Leadership: A Journey into the Nature of Legitimate Power and Greatness *(1977)*

When you *Lead with Your Life*, you must have a desire to live as a servant leader. Servant leaders who are successful have incredible people skills. They effectively know how to pay attention to the people and colleagues they serve to help them reach their maximum potential on a daily basis. Servant leaders work hard to understand the needs of their internal and external customers so they can better provide the services that each customer needs.

In this book, *Lead with Your Life*, we have explored six principles prior to the principle of being servant leaders. Of the many principles that a great leader possesses, the principle of becoming a servant to the people one leads is the most important. The desire to serve others isn't a to-do-list item for great leaders. It is simply who the leader is. Serving others is what each of us was created to do. Voluntary servitude is what gives life meaning and significance.

Do not mistake leaders who desire to serve others as being people who are soft or weak. They have the skills, expertise, and courage to make tough decisions without hesitation. They truly care about other people, and they find extreme joy in helping them to grow and maximize their potential. As a leader, you can measure your effectiveness as a servant by asking a few simple questions: "Are the people that I am are serving growing as individuals? While being served by me, are they gaining knowledge, becoming better mentally and physically, and likely to become servants to others as well?" When you lead from the front with your life, you want the answers to these questions to be a resounding "Yes."

As a servant leader, you have to make growth in others a key part of your strategy for making the organization, family, team, colleagues, or business better. Growth in others is more than a win-win. When the people you serve find fulfillment, the capacity of the organization, business, or family grows, which, in turn, leads to a greater ability to enhance the service given to internal and external customers. Simply put, your organization will start to do things better and explore and do things that it was never able to do before. So the servant leader principle actually leads to a win-win-win!

The ultimate goal of a servant leader is to make the world a better place. He or she operates from a belief that there is enough for everyone. Successful leaders focus on developing everyone throughout the organization and beyond to reach his or her full potential. Servant leaders inspire and encourage people; they do not use people. Servant leaders' goals are always to create a winning environment where trust and respect are staples of the organization. Great leaders have a genuine concern for the well-being of each and every internal and external customer who has a stake in the organization. Servant leaders practice humility because they know it's not about them; instead, it's about helping other people grow into their purposes. When you lead with your life, you spend your time building bridges for others to cross. You get out front and clear the way for your team members to make it to the other side safely.

Leading with your life means you care about every individual with whom you interact. You create an environment that people want to be a part of. Organizations that serve their internal and external customers with the goal of achieving 100-percent satisfaction usually achieve incredible success.

The next sections of this chapter will discuss in more detail the characteristics of servant leaders.

OUTSTANDING LEADERS OF ORGANIZATIONS CREATE HEALTHY ENVIRONMENTS

Successful organizations are led by servant leaders who focus on four particular principles:

1. Creating an environment of trust and respect—a place where positive treatment and encouragement of everyone are the norms. Employees are shown from day one that they have value within the organization.

2. Creating individualized growth and development programs that lead to promotions and advancement within the organization. These organizations emphasize the importance of continuing education and skills training for each individual so personal and professional growth opportunities are a real possibility.

3. Training internal customers for the future of the organization, not only for what the employee is doing today. Being a visionary and being on the cutting edge allow growth opportunities for everyone.

4. Focusing on the whole person, so leaders see each team member not just as a worker but as a person. Leaders reward the behavior that they would like to see more of and empower team members at every level to make decisions, especially the team members who work closest to the front line, that is, those who work closest to serving external customers.

As a servant leader, when you master and incorporate the four principles above into your daily routine, the end result is likely to be an organization that has a winning culture because of less turnover: people will really enjoy coming to work! When people enjoy what they do, they become better listeners to their internal and external customers. Better listeners will hear about and then create the products, services, and programs that the internal and external customers need. Fulfilling customers' needs results in greater customer loyalty for using the products, services, and programs of the organization; their loyalty allows you to grow those customers more and expand new customer bases.

Servant leaders know that nurturing long-term relationships is key to organizational success year in and year out. There is no room for complacency or coasting. With each day, challenges and opportunities come to the organization and each team member. This is why when it comes to their internal and external customers, servant leaders listen, hear, plan, take action, and repeat these steps. Building value in others is what serving is all about.

Serving others, like anything else, is a skill that can be developed. Leaders who are great servants became that way by working at it. Think of the people you consider to be great servant leaders and consider the following seven principles that reflect outstanding "people skills" and see if they have them. Chances are your answers will be "Yes!"

OUTSTANDING LEADERS HAVE EXCELLENT PEOPLE SKILLS

All great leaders have developed the following seven people skills:

1. Listening. Servant leaders are active listeners. By listening well, these leaders are able to identify the needs of their internal and external customers. When you can identify the needs of others, it is a lot easier to create and execute plans that will meet and exceed the customers' needs.

2. **Self-Confidence / Self-Awareness.** Servant leaders know themselves well, but more importantly, they know what they will never be. When you know your value, you will always have a voice. Your self-confidence and self-awareness are directly proportionate to your preparation and knowledge of the situation. Chance always favors the prepared, and you are only as good as you believe you are.

3. **Openness to the Possibilities.** Servant leaders are not know-it-alls. It's so easy when you are the leader to get caught up into thinking that you know it all, but servant leaders turn this train of thought on its head. They are open to what others say and think and create a team of thinkers all around them. Servant leaders are not interested in "yes" people; they are interested in the best people.

4. **Leadership Development.** Servant Leaders know that growth comes through education, opportunities, and letting go. They equip their people with the right information and resources and then let them run with it. As a leader, if both of your hands are full, you can't pick anything else up, so you have to hand things over to others if you want to stay out front and continue to grow others.

5. **Good Coaching.** Servant leaders focus on mentoring and coaching others. They develop others by engaging and inspiring each team member to be an active part in the overall success of the team. Good coaches don't belittle or control team members; instead, they inspire, encourage, and stay positive no matter the situation.

6. **Empowering Others.** Servant leaders let people be their best. They trust each team member to do what they were brought on to do and then some. Servant leaders encourage everyone to shine bright, because maximum potential achieved by everyone means maximum success achieved in the world. Their goal is always to make the world a better place.

7. Visionaries. Servant leaders are visionaries. They look ahead much further than their eyes can see. As a leader, if you lack vision, you will eventually fail. Without vision you simply react to situations instead of predicting and planning for what could happen. This means eventually you will make bad decisions, which may cost the organization and your people everything. Visionaries are proactive. They understand how to prevent the organization and its people from getting into high-risk or precarious situations.

To become a better servant leader, you need to develop and implement the four principles found in effective leaders of organizations, together with these seven principles found in those with outstanding people skills daily. Remember that success at anything is a result of repetition, repetition, repetition.

Scribbles and Doodles

As a leader, who are you serving, and how can you best serve others? (family, friends, colleagues, and customers)

_____
_____
_____
_____
_____
_____
_____
_____
_____
_____
_____
_____

List five ways you are making your own unique contributions to better serve others personally and professionally.

___

In what ways are you getting better each day serving others personally and professionally? And are you getting better each day personally and professionally?

___

Final Thoughts:

Summary

Leadership can be defined as a function of guidance and direction. Successful teams have outstanding leadership. They have an individual or individuals who lead with their lives. Winning teams win because their leaders understand that true leadership means taking action, not simply taking a position. Successful teams have leaders who find resources and answers that inspire and elevate each member of the team. They create a winning environment and communicate a vision that everyone is eager to follow.

Outstanding leaders have a vision not just for today but for five and ten years down the road. These leaders share their vision with everyone on the team. Great team leaders are visible and accessible. They take a genuine interest in their people. They want to know if team members are meeting their personal goals as well as the team's goals. They look for ways to bring out the best in every individual because the team can only win if everyone is executing his or her role. Leaders who live by the philosophy, "Treat everyone right, but don't dare treat them the same," will always maximize the potential of everyone on their teams. All members want to feel they are valuable and are adding value to the team.

> "The people who get on in this world are the people who get up and look for the circumstances they want, and, if they can't find them, make them."
>
> —*George Bernard Shaw was awarded the Nobel Prize in Literature for his plays and literary and political commentaries and an Academy Award for the filmscript of his drama* "Pygmalion," *which was later adapted for the musical* "My Fair Lady."

Great leaders make their own luck. They attract the things and people they want in their lives. Successful leadership takes courage to risk it all for the art of possibility. Teams that are constantly among the best are the teams with leaders who know the way, show the way, and go the way for their people. They are led by people who are knowledgeable and skilled in getting the best out of every member of the team.

> "Perhaps the most valuable result of all education is the ability to make yourself do the thing you have to do, when it ought to be done, whether you like it or not."
>
> —*Walter Bagehot, nineteenth-century editor of the magazine* The Economist,- *English banker, writer, and political philosopher.*

That's self-discipline; that's leadership.

Scribbles and Doodles

Leadership: What you do speaks so loudly that I cannot hear what you say.

Write your thoughts about this statement:

_____
_____
_____
_____
_____
_____
_____

Leadership is turning people on through proper inspiration so they can achieve their maximum potential in the game of life.

Write your thoughts:

_____
_____
_____

Leadership teaches; excellence is not an exception. It is the prevailing attitude that in order to achieve the big things, you develop a solid foundation in little things.

Write your thoughts:

Leadership is not a position, privilege, or title. It is a responsibility to the people you serve.

Write your thoughts:

Final Thoughts:

About the Author

Motivation, noun. Incentive, drive.
Motive, noun. Something that causes a person to act. A stimulus to action. Motive implies an emotion or desire operating on the will and causing it to act.

While *Merriam-Webster's Dictionary* gives us these definitions of motivation and motive in words, Almon Gunter defines motivation by his actions. Almon's aspiration is for all individuals to possess the desire, dedication, and determination to succeed in achieving their goals. His formula for success involves diehard dedication, never-ending enthusiasm, hard work, heart, and hustle, with the end result of becoming an MVP in the game of life.

Almon Gunter is the CEO/President of Almon Gunter Motivates, Inc. He is a highly acclaimed motivational, inspirational public speaker, author, and consultant, as well as a world-class sprinter in U.S. Track and Field. He uses his experiences on the track and as a business executive to help inspire others in the game of life.

Almon Gunter is a no-fluff force of nature who focuses on mental and physical fitness. His role is to help every individual discover his or her potential. He helps individuals find their most effective tools and refine them into razor-sharp instruments so they can compete in the greatest game of all—life. Almon believes that every individual is born with a purpose to fulfill. He encourages everyone he meets to *Dream It. Dare It. Do It.*

Acknowledgments

Special thanks to my children: Ola, Almon III, and Austin, and to my five grandchildren: Nyasia, Seymone, William, Londynn, and Leighla. Just as a bundle of sticks tightly tied together cannot be broken, we as a family working together as a team cannot be broken. Choose the road less traveled and blaze new trails always. Don't be afraid to build bridges, knowing that some of the bridges you build will not be for you to cross, but for others to cross. Great leaders serve others. To my sister Amanda and brother Dwayne, I love you dearly. We have it all because we have each other.

Dennis Webber, I honor and respect you as a brother, friend, mentor, leader, and trusted advisor. You constantly lead from the front, and you are everything a great leader should strive to be. Glad to be in the fight with you. To my Baby Brother Greg Dorsey, what an honor to have you in my life. So grateful and blessed to be able to share information and learn, risk, and grow daily with you. Together we will serve people and build bridges for others. I'm glad to be powered by Astoryo and the Almon Gunter Experience (AGE) Team, Dallas Smith, Kevin Cox, and Shelda Moll. Aaron Harris (Big A), you're like a son to me. So proud of you for all the work you do mentoring and leading today's youth in a positive direction. You are an incredible role model. Alan Louder, you are a diamond, my friend. What an incredible leader and role model you are. Glad to work with you to help maximize the potential in others. Kirk Farber, so proud to have spent the last two decades with you working with today's youth. We might not help all of them, but we are going to keep working at it for sure!

Shelda Moll (Shell Bell), all I can say is you are the best! For over ten years your support and belief in my mission, vision, and goal have been unwavering. So grateful that you are on my team. Grace, thanks for reminding me that what I do matters.

As always, a sincere thanks to my incredible brothers from another mother: Windle (Peck), Earriet (Easy), and Byron Lee for always being there for me no matter what. Byron, you keep me hungry and grinding because you live your life like I live mine: Every Day Is Game Day! Also, thank you to Ricky Battle, who is always there with an encouraging word. Tommy Sampson, you bigggg . . ., you know I love you to life brother! To my dear friend CJ, you are always there reminding me that we all have the power to do great things. Go Noles! Bruce Canady, please know that your friendship is greatly appreciated.

There are so many others who helped me along the way, and I say, thank you. No one achieves success alone, and I am grateful for all of the help I receive from so many on a daily basis. I am grateful for the love, and I will continue to learn, risk, and grow. Always *Lead with Your Life*!

For more information on other products by Almon W. Gunter, Jr.

KEYNOTE
BOOKS
TRAINING CAMPS
CONSULTING

Please Contact
Almon Gunter Motivates, Inc.
Post Office Box 194
Jacksonville, FL 32234
Office Phone: 904.803.1917
Website: www.almongunterexperience.com
Via-email: almon@almonguntermotivates.com
Twitter: @almongunter
Facebook: Almon Gunter
Instagram: almongunter
LinkedIn: Almon Gunter

Give AGM a call today, so you can live the **Super Freak Way** and **Focus To Win!**

www.ingramcontent.com/pod-product-compliance
Lightning Source LLC
Chambersburg PA
CBHW030455010526
44118CB00011B/956